MADD TRUTH

*Lasting Lessons for
Students of Life*

MADD TRUTH

Lasting Lessons for Students of Life

by:

DR. ALFONSO WYATT

Strategic Destiny
DESIGNING FUTURES THROUGH FAITH & FACTS

Strategic Destiny books may be purchased through booksellers.

Cataloging-in-Publication Data is on file with the Library of Congress.

ISBN: 978-0-9982566-0-3 (paperback)

Library of Congress Control Number: 2017911290

Interior and Cover Designs: Taneki Dacres of The Vine Publishing, Inc.

Printed in the United States of America.

ACKNOWLEDGEMENTS

EXPRESSION OF GRATITUDE

To the incredible credible messengers in NYC and around the country working to keep young people safe and free. May these words help heal and inspire as you heal and inspire.

To John H. Bess (RIP), the best youth developer on the planet; The Valley staff and Robesons who made it to the mountaintop. To Clinton Lacey and Julie Peterson for your bold vision to use a youth development and mentoring approach, to reach court-adjudicated youth and young adults, through the creation of the Arches program.

To CC-FY/Bronx Connect staff for teaching how to mentor, guide and counsel court adjudicated youth and concomitantly growing the field.

To Dr. C. V. Mason for your early vision and inspiration to hire and train Uth Turn North Campus mentors to work with youth.

To Carolyn Grimstead, all my Mental Ninjas, my many mentee sons and daughters, NYC Cure Violence Staff, Institute for Transformative Mentoring staff and graduates.

To my wife and chief encourager, Ouida C. Wyatt.

THANK YOU.

TABLE OF CONTENTS

FOREWORD

D r. Alfonso Wyatt, the "Godfather" of youth development, has once again put pen to paper in service of our nation's most vulnerable youth, families, and communities. In the wake of the recent shift in the national political landscape, the need for bold and innovative leadership has never been greater. The old models of reaching and teaching disconnected, criminalized, demonized, and largely abandoned youth, that cycle in and out of the justice system, have all failed.

A new movement of indigenous community leadership, known as Credible Messenger Mentoring, is on the rise. Rooted, relevant, passionate, experienced and skilled credible messengers stand at the threshold of transformation as they use themselves as the tools to engage, encourage and empower our youth and families that continue to be marginalized and dehumanized.

It is in this context that he provides both inspirational vision and wise counsel to this growing movement. He helps to unveil the greatness within credible messengers, as well as the youth they serve, and both their particular value in today's time. He warns readers, and us all, not to wallow in past pathology but to use even the worst of experiences as lessons and launching pads for unfolding healing and progress.

Bro. Wyatt points to Truth as both the vehicle and the North Star that must guide the credible messenger to experience and facilitate transformation so they may do the same in youth in their charge. Ultimately, Dr. Wyatt calls all to discard the trappings of fear, false pride and indifference as he summons us to pick up our cross and dare to be great in the face of adversity. *Madd Truth: Lasting Lessons For Students of Life* is an extraordinary and timely message for extraordinary times.

~ Clinton Lacey
Director, Department Youth Rehabilitative Services
Washington, DC

INTRODUCTION

I want to tell you the truth about the truth as it relates to life, people, decisions, spirit and yourself. The truth is what it is, even if you refuse to recognize it, agree with it, or follow it. The truth does not need batteries, but it can give energy. The truth is not food, but it can surely feed you. The truth is not a knife, but it can cut through fantasy and lies. The truth never went to school, but it can give a first rate "life" education. The truth never lived, but it can explain life to you. A person can try to ditch, deny, or dog out the truth, but no matter, it will still be the truth.

You probably heard the saying that the truth can set you free, but before it can do that, it must first find you, and then get in you. I must caution you there is a price for seeking as well as avoiding the truth—you have to decide which price you want to pay. Can you spot people who have rejected truth living in a blurred world where it is hard to know what is real and what is made-up? To tell the truth, living a lie is much harder than owning up to the truth.

You will note throughout this book what I refer to as "wisdom statements." Highlight the statements that speak to your soul. Meditate on these *truths*. A comprehensive list of truism is also provided at the end of the book. In addition, use the blank pages at the end of each chapter to make notes or write your own truth. While we may not have been introduced, I want you to know that I love and respect you, so much so, that I vow to tell you the truth, the whole truth, and nothing but the truth as I understand it.

So now, I want to tell you the truth about me. I am not a young man (just young at heart). I have over 40 years (yes I am old—but very wise if I have to say so myself) of experience working with teens and young adults from: probation, group homes, foster care, youth programs, colleges, public, private schools, GED students, charter schools, churches, gangs, addiction programs, homeless shelters, juvenile detention facilities, jails and prisons. I have worked with the talented, the motivated, and the hard to motivate; with the excited and depressed; with the lost and found; the locked up and free. I have learned from my work (and from living) that it is not always easy to deal with, hold on to, or find the truth. Nevertheless, it is never far away. Some would say that the truth lives inside of you. Now don't get nervous, this is not a "spooky" book; the truth should never scare you.

People who really love you will speak the truth to you, even if it may hurt you. It is not always easy being real with self or others. I know firsthand what it feels like to run from the truth—all I can say is it is a race that you will never win. Sometimes a person who loves and respects you enough to tell you the truth may be thought of as a hater—that is NOT true. A hater is a person who feeds lies to you and wants you to believe it is the truth because he or she is trying to trip you up, or hold you down.

In order for our time to be productive, let me suggest that you open yourself up and not hide from the truth. Don't be afraid to see the real you. The truth may hurt at times, but believe me, once embraced, it can become your best friend and dependable lifelong guide. With this said, are you ready to take your journey that has the power to transform your thinking, behavior, and life?

SECTION **1**
OBSERVATION

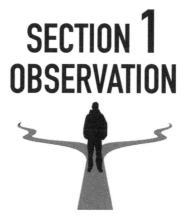

OH SAY CAN YOU SEE?

I t is possible to look at the outside "image" of a person but not see the "real" inside person. Come on, tell the truth, you've been fooled by someone who seemed '*fo real*,' but turned out to be faker than fake. Perhaps you let your emotions cloud your eyes and you could not see the truth about this person. Maybe you got use to making excuses for the person, and over time, you began to believe the unbelievable. If you are ever going to "*see*" truth, you have to stop "*looking*" at it.

Let me see if I can make this point plain. A good window washer does not look through the glass that he or she has just cleaned. If you "look" through the glass, you cannot "see" the missed spots and streaks on the surface of the glass. You have to "see" what is on the surface of the glass without looking through the glass. Are you getting it?

Let's try another example. A mirror allows you to look at your reflection, but that does not automatically mean you see the real you. When you look at objects or people, you notice how they appear. Seeing is several steps beyond looking. When you begin to see, one is not distracted by what merely looks good. What is pleasing to the eye may not always be pleasing for you. Are you beginning to see what I mean?

Have you ever heard of insight? Insight is the ability to see yourself in different situations. Most people have no problem 'peepin' other people's stuff. You know the type who has the 411 on everybody else. This same person is often clueless when the light is on them. A person without insight can't see how they are hurting themselves or others by their actions (or inactions). A person without insight finds it difficult to learn from their mistakes. People, young and old, who do not have insight are limited by their inner-blindness. It is impossible to help a person who can't see any need for help.

Please do not blind yourself to yourself. You should know that no matter how deep your game, how much shade you try to put on your stuff, or how undercover you may wish to operate, someone is always able to see the real you. Grab hold to the fact, you will meet people who are not what they appear to be, it is your job to keep looking until you see the real person.

For example, the so-called thug may not want others to know he (or she) has been hurt in past relationships so he plays the 'get you before you can get me game.' Some people refuse to let their "soft" side show because they do not want to be played, or be considered a "non ruff neck" by their peers, or others who may mistake kindness for weakness.

There is good news. You can develop insight. It takes hard work and personal honesty (remember don't ever fool yourself). Insight is a gift that can help you stop looking at others and start seeing yourself. You have to see you for who you really are and not how you wish to appear. Are you ready to take an inward journey? Find a quiet place and be still for several minutes, close your eyes and take a few deep breaths to begin to focus. See yourself in good times. See yourself when you struggled. See yourself when you were proud.

Now see yourself when disappointed. See when you triumphed over a problem. See when a problem got the best of you. See what others see in you. Look at yourself the way you see yourself, and know, it is all you, the good, bad and yes, even the ugly. Decide if you want to keep up appearances, or really work on yourself. Don't get bent out of shape because of what you may see inside, think of yourself as an unfinished work of art and vow to keep on painting until the masterpiece is done.

MADD TRUTH REFLECTIONS

_____

_____

_____

_____

_____

_____

_____

_____

_____

_____

_____

_____

_____

_____

_____

_____

_____

_____

SHOULDAH WOULDAH COULDAH PEOPLE

I have met people who are trying to do the impossible by wasting their lives trying to change the past. This is like trying to grab the wind, or shovel smoke—it can't be done, no matter how hard you try. You may be able to change your looks, eye color, hairstyle, nail color, 'hood,' friends, schools, or colors, but you can't change yesterday even if it is messing you up today. 'Shouldah, wouldah, couldah' people spend most of their waking hours lost in endless "what ifs." They talk about how they 'shouldah' stayed in school, or in or out of this or that relationship. They moan about how they 'couldah' had a job last year if they had not run into their friend and decided to 'hang' rather than interview. It is sad to see a person, young or old, stuck on yesterday's bad luck life glue trap.

So how do you get free from the invisible grip of the past? That is the right question. The answer is LET IT GO. Your past is not holding you back; check it out, the past has no hands. Ask yourself (and tell the truth), am I the one who is actually clinging to the past? It is time to make a decision. It is time to get unstuck. It is time to get rid of your favorite reasons (excuses) for not making it, for not trying, or for giving up. It is time to let go of past pain. It is time, right now, to let go of lingering anger, nagging doubts, failed attempts and troubling disappointments. Let go of unpleasant memories that can only discourage, deflate and depress you. If the past is a drag, and it is not serving you well, you have the right to ask why am I serving it?

I challenge you to go back in your mind to when you were

hurt; when a mess-up messed you up, when damaging words were spoken. Now, unhook yourself from the anger, depression, disappointment or pain that is haunting you. You don't have to live in "Replayville" one day longer. No power can change the past because what's done is done. It is time to stop looking backward and walking forward, that's why you are bumping into things.

Turn around, face the direction you are headed and take charge of your present. You may have to forgive yourself before you take this journey. You may even have to forgive a person who has hurt you before you can get started. Please know that forgiveness is not about who was right or wrong, it means you are ready to move on with your life. You can and must learn from the past, but you don't have to live in the past. It is time to turn the 'shouldah, wouldah, couldahs' into 'I dids'—I did go back to school; I did get a job; I did stop getting high; I did learn how to love myself more than my pain. Here is some wisdom you can take to the bank: a smart way to positively impact your future is to successfully learn from your past.

MADD TRUTH REFLECTIONS

_____

_____

_____

_____

_____

_____

_____

_____

_____

_____

_____

_____

_____

_____

_____

_____

_____

_____

FOOLS IN DA HOOD

Have you ever met grown folk who seem to never tire of hanging out? You see these "old wonders" everyday. They hang on the same street corners with people way younger. Their hats are turned backward and their pants are 'saggin.'" They eat pizza, potato chips, hot wings, and curly fries, just like everyone else on the block. The old women's skirts are as high, and their shorts are as short as the rest of the younger sisters. They get their hair done in the same amazing styles and colors as their younger peers.

These adults don't seem to work, nor have many pressing appointments (except when called "downtown") that pull them away from the "sacred" corner. One can say that they are star graduates of 'shouldah, wouldah, couldah university.' These professional hang-out artists will tell you, and anyone else in earshot, great stories about when they were on top. What is scary is that these folk are someone's brother, sister, mother, father and tragically, grandparents. Something is wrong with this picture. What would make a grown person willingly stunt their growth and hang with and around people who could be their children?

The answer is deeper than they want to stay forever young, forever down, or the response for everything these days, namely, 'keepin' it real.' Somewhere along the line, they refused to change. They have this strange ability to see themselves as slicker than slick (old school saying). They are, unfortunately, 'fools in da hood' who may grow old, but will never mature. When you were a child, you thought as a child, you reasoned as a child, you acted and reacted as a child, but if you are to mature, you have to make a decision to put away childish things.

Now the question is what will you be doing years from now? Will you take the place of the old people on the street? No one makes a plan to waste his or her life. No one wishes to become the biggest bum or 'bummette' in the world. Some people, become residents on 'Nowhere Boulevard' due in part to low aspiration, laziness, hardheadedness, negative peers and magical thinking.

Have you ever heard of magical thinking? This is when a person is messing up but they hold on to the belief (fantasy) that they can get themselves together anytime they want as if by magic. They state, "I can stop drinking tomorrow." "I can stop stealing when I get enough money to go straight." "I can get high and still get by." "I can pass in school even though I am always passing by the school." "I can save time by wasting time." "I can stop seeing my 'boo' (try boo-hoo) who beats me." We tell ourselves lies, but it does not change the truth it just postpones it for a while. It is sad to see or know somebody who has ruined their life. It is worse when the person is you.

Please don't think I am being mean by calling people who live to hang on the street fools. It is not my intent to disrespect people. I realize there are many stories, issues, policies, family situations and injustices that can assist in ruining a person's life. With that said, unfortunately, some people may hang on the corner until death, sickness (mental, physical or spiritual) or an arrest removes them; or they move to another corner, or they finally wake up and take responsibility for their future. Do not put your life on hold waiting for the right time to get yourself together; the right time is NOW. If you look for 'been there done that folk,' know that they can be trustworthy life guides.

MADD TRUTH REFLECTIONS

_____

_____

_____

_____

_____

_____

_____

_____

_____

_____

_____

_____

_____

_____

_____

_____

_____

_____

_____

_____

4

'HOW YA LIVIN'?

I remember talking to men at the Bowery Mission, a New York homeless shelter on what was once called skid row. The Bowery Mission is where men live when they have hit rock bottom. This place is where dreams struggle to be reborn, or may eventually die. The men living in the Bowery Mission are somebody's father, son, uncle, brother, cousin, or friend. The stories they told about their slide into darkness varies; however, a constant theme was drug and alcohol abuse and incarceration.

The brothers talked about how they discovered (too late) that they were not getting high, but in reality, they were getting low. So low, they had to cash bottles and cans for a living. So low that bathing, fresh clothes, or brushing one's teeth was not even a thought anymore. So low that they cease to be human beings in the eyes of people who ride trains, eat in café sidewalks, walk the streets, or pass laws. Does this sound like fun to anyone?

One man who grew up in Chicago said he never thought the day would come when he would be living in an "abandominium" (a discarded cardboard refrigerator box) under a highway. He thought, for some reason, that he could out-slick life. He felt his once good looks, serious connections, and street smarts would allow him to walk down a path of self-destruction and somehow not be destroyed (magical thinking once again).

I recall another story told to me by a young man, while under the spell of crack saying he would only eat good garbage from rich neighborhoods. This allowed him to feel superior to the other 'poor bums' who ate low class local garbage. Your mind can play deep tricks on you, especially when it attempts to make wrong right. Your thoughts have power; that is precisely why you must be mindful of what is on your mind.

Let me ask you this question, when you get older, do you plan to live in a house, apartment, shelter or in an abandominium? This question either made you laugh, think, or get angry. If you can't take care of yourself, if you give up on yourself, if you expect others to live your life for you, you have my permission to go book your reservation for your abandominium. No one makes a plan to ruin his or her life; in most cases, it is a slow slide down a very slippery pole.

My advice to these men was, you may have fallen, you may have been knocked down, but it is your responsibility, your duty, to get up, dust yourself off, learn from your mistakes, and get going. If you want more out of life, you will not find it at the bottom of a bottle, at the end of a 'blunt,' in pills (this is not ecstasy), inhaling powdered coke/heroin, huffing, tripping, or using a needle.

Sisters, please don't think that only men ruin their lives. Nothing could be further from the truth. Destruction is an equal opportunity destroyer. It does not respect gender, age, sexual orientation, if your pockets are full, or if you are dead broke, or whether you got your own hair, bought some, or if you were just finished dancing in a video.

Do you know that the incarceration rate on ratio for women is rising faster than for males? The common tale told by women in jail and prison is, how drugs, and men who used or sold drugs, messed them up. Crack probably did more to harm women in the eyes of family and society than any other drug in the whole history of drugging. This drug caused mothers to abandon their children in numbers never before seen. Crack turned female users into desperate freaks who used sex as their neighborhood credit card. I told you that sometimes the truth hurts.

Women who depend on their looks to get what they want from men can be in for a rude awakening. No matter how good you look, how tight your stuff may be, somebody will come along who looks as pretty, or better than you. If your significant other kicks you to the curb and you have no skills, no keys, no ambition, other than to be a kept woman, you have placed yourself in a position to depend on a person for life's basics, namely, food, clothing and shelter. No one, except a baby, should be that dependent on another person. Believe me, choices made from desperation usually come back to haunt you.

I know a person who counsels girls as young as 12 years old who are tricking for someone who tricked them. Pimps have the unique ability to spot desperation and weakness in the eyes of their victims. There is nothing glamorous about having sex with strangers, who may have sexually transmitted diseases like herpes, gonorrhea, syphilis or HIV/AIDS. Only to turn over the money to someone whose words say they love you, but whose behavior shouts: "You ain't nothing but a meal ticket baby."

I have seen working sisters support men who won't work. These women clock-in at their jobs while their partners hang out on the corner, harassing other women, scheming, sneaking and getting high until their "meal ticket" returns. The question must be asked how do you really want to live? Take time to think about your answer.

Imagine it is 10 years from now and a story about your life appears in the newspaper. Write a paragraph about what was said about you. Write about your hopes, dreams and accomplishments. Who are the people in your life; what do you do to make a living; where do you live; and what kind of car do you drive? If you don't feel like writing you can use your phone and video, rap, draw, record your response, or just think about what actions you must take to make your dreams come true.

MADD TRUTH REFLECTIONS

5

BEEN THERE... DONE THAT...

If you have ever hurt yourself or others by your thoughts, words or deeds, please know that you are not alone. Don't let frustration, or other people tell you that you are useless, hopeless, or less than them. There are people you can talk to who have messed up big time, and through hard work, have managed to turn their lives around. These credible messengers may have been to prison, may have been in and out of drug rehab, may have been homeless, poor, dropped out of school, stayed on the corner, yet these same folks are successful today.

These sisters and brothers have battled depression, all manner of abuse, and have fought against the odds, predictions, and low expectations of others. They have leaped over obstacles, punishing policies and self-doubt. They now proudly stand as productive citizens. These are the real heroes and sheroes 'in *da hood*' who got tired of hanging, banging, and playing dangerous games with their lives. You should ask these credible messengers how they made it out of Hell? Their real response to your real question is what '*keepin'* it *real*' should really mean.

Many credible messengers are counselors in programs, mentors, neighbors, teachers, religious people, business owners, family members and friends who have escaped from 'Hopelessville.' These people are "star" graduates of the school of hard knocks. If you want wisdom, go to the wise, if you want to be fooled then ask a fool.

If you look for some 'been there done that folk,' they can be trustworthy life guides. It has been proven that a caring adult can help turn around the life of a young person. I am not telling you to hand your life over to someone else. If your would be mentor tries to take advantage of you by misusing what he or she knows about you, that person is not a true mentor. They are self-centered, manipulative and can be dangerous.

If you need a caring mentor in your life, you should look for these qualities: patience, wisdom, truthfulness and consistent behavior that state that your life, words and dreams matter. Please know there are been there done that people and never been there and never done that people that you can talk to and get inspiration as well as direction.

Every person who learns how to drive a car must master how to make a U Turn. You usually make this type of maneuver after you discover you are heading in the wrong direction. The beauty of a U Turn is that you turn away from what you discover is the wrong way, and turn toward the right direction. Look at credible messengers as driving instructors along the road of life helping folk make U Turns.

Not one person who draws breath can truthfully say that he or she made it on their own; everybody needs help; a word of encouragement; support, or just a friendly ear. There are people who can open doors for you yet you must make up your mind to go through on your own. There are people who will try to hook you up—you must allow them. There are people who will try to mess you up—you must avoid them. Over time you will be able to identify '*fo' real*' been there done that people that can be helpful to you. Learn from their mistakes and success as you benefit from the incredible knowledge of credible messengers.

MADD TRUTH REFLECTIONS

_____

_____

_____

_____

_____

_____

_____

_____

_____

_____

_____

_____

_____

_____

_____

_____

_____

_____

_____

6

WHAT'S REALLY NEW?

f you witness an event for the first time in your life, that makes it new right? The real answer is yes and perhaps no (this is the stuff that makes life tricky). Just because something is new to you, does not necessarily mean that it has never happened before. For example, hard times ain't new. Self-destruction ain't new. Drugs ain't new. A *bumpin'* beat ain't new. People looking good, but up to no good ain't new. Growing up without a father ain't new. People gettin' locked up over and over again ain't new.

Young people having babies ain't new. Hustling instead of working ain't new. Dropping out of school ain't new. Racism ain't new. Selling drugs and riding around in nice cars ain't new. Dressing up to stand on the corner 24/7 ain't new. Being lied to by a person you never thought would lie ain't new. Blonde hair (dyed or bought) ain't new. Carrying a gun ain't new. Gangs ain't new. Worshipping stars and wanting to be one ain't new. Wanting something, but giving nothing to get it ain't new. Usin' ain't ain't new. And droppin 'g's off of the end of words ain't new...'*Um jes sayin.*'

Don't be fooled; life will always present something as new. Taking heroin (please don't take it) for example is not new. It may seem hip (another old school word) for young people in the '*burbs or '*da hood*' who think they are rebelling, want to be down, or expressing their individuality by snorting or shooting dope. Heroin was a danger then and it is a danger now. I saw firsthand what drugs did to people, families and cities. It sucked the life, joy, vitality and sense of safety out of communities, and replaced it with fear, hatred, suspicion, devastation and death.

Most of you are old enough to remember what crack did in its heyday. This cocaine based drug created monsters who roamed the streets, day and night, stealing and selling whatever they could—all for a high that was gone seemingly with the smoke. What was new was that crack was marketed to young people and women. We are still feeling the effects of children (80's Babies) forced to raise themselves because their parents where incapable, missing in action, incarcerated, or died. Now, there is a surge in overdoses all around the country caused by pain-killers, like oxycontin, or fentanyl.

On a lighter note, I remember when I pierced my ear back in the day. Mother Wyatt was not having it. Was I expressing my individuality or was I doing what my "cool" peers did? While piercing other parts of the body may seem new, if we travel to other countries, we would see that the people pierce what many would think should not be pierced. Tattoos are not new. Old sailors had mermaids, ships, their mother or girlfriend's name placed on their forearms, chest, and back. In Japan, tattooing the whole body is considered a sacred art form (this has been going on for centuries).

I would be a hypocrite if I did not acknowledge that there is something exciting about being first; being different and marching to your own beat. I must say that wearing your hair short or long (big ole Afro's are back!) in braids, dyed, fried, or laid to side, will not guarantee that you will make it in life. You should never confuse style (fads) over substance. You may love that homeless look, but you don't have to live on the street. You may like the druggie look, but you don't have to become an addict. You have the right to make any statement that you wish with your body, clothing, nail polish, or hair, but don't allow what was intended to be a statement of your uniqueness to mess up your life.

You can tattoo Chinese characters on your arm, neck, ankle or private parts if you wish, but at the very least, find out what is written on your skin. You can have your name, your boo's name or your posse's name printed on the base of your neck (but remember you may break up, move on—or change). You can get your gang's name, street number, teardrop, or motto ('born to lose' was a favorite several generations ago) placed on your body that will cost big money should you decide later on in life to get it removed.

A famous group in the 60's (back in my day) recorded a song with this hook: "It's your thing, do what you wanna do..." What was missing in the lyrics is that there are consequences for actions taken or not taken in life. Please don't get lost in fads and forget all about substance. Even if you rock the latest gear, if you can drop it like it is real hot, if you know all the latest sayings, or you can spit rhymes like no other... none of it matters if you can't read, write, or take care of yourself.

I don't want you to grow old standing on the corner with your tattooed self, grinning through a faded grill, lost in your yesterdays. This kind of life can get boring: going upstairs; then back downstairs; with a few interruptions to go to the store; bathroom, eat at Red Lobster; dance (or fight) at the club; go to Great Adventure or end up doing bids.

Have fun while you are young, but know that you will be older a lot longer than you will be young and you owe it to yourself to work from that truth. The statement all things in moderation may apply especially when it comes to dealing with what's new. There is very little that is new under the sun just new thoughts about old ideas.

MADD TRUTH REFLECTIONS

SECTION 2
INVESTMENT

WHAT MONEY CAN'T BUY

I t is has been said that the love of money is the root of all evil. Some people will lie, cheat, rob and kill for money. Money in this country means status. You are automatically thought to be important if you got money. If you are broke, nobody wants to know you. Just because you wear designer clothes does not mean that you also take on the designer's lifestyle (thanks largely to your fashion support). There are some well-dressed poor folk driven by the idea that image is everything. I am not saying that you should not want to look nice or desire nice things, but know that there are some important things in life that money can't buy.

FONZO'S TOP TEN: WHAT MONEY CAN'T BUY

1. Genuine happiness

2. Peace of mind

3. A real friend

4. More time on your life's clock

5. Good health

6. Common sense (there are plenty of wealthy fools)

7. The desire to go after something worthwhile in life

8. A better/different past

9. Self-esteem (if you hate yourself while poor you'll hate yourself when rich)

10. A real, true and lasting love...there in good times and bad, for richer or poorer, in sickness and in health (you can always find someone who loves what you can do for them... they are a dime a dozen).

(Please add to this list things that money can't buy).

Please don't think you should not want money. However, getting and spending money should never be the sole pursuit of your life. You may have seen some of your peers who became famous. Shortly after '*blowin' up*,' some had to declare bankruptcy (more money going out than money coming in), because the good times rolled over them. It is one thing to be poor and wish you were rich. It is another thing altogether to have been rich and become poor.

It is not enough to know how to make money, a person should also know how to make money grow through sound investments. The Biggie Smalls and Tupac Shakur drama was truly a modern hip-hop tragedy. Here were two rich and talented young men with so much to live for, with people who loved them, and dreams yet to be born, and now both are d-e-a-d! Their money was not enough to buy peace and happiness. Money can change the external, but it will not automatically change the internal.

MADD TRUTH REFLECTIONS

_____

_____

_____

_____

_____

_____

_____

_____

_____

_____

_____

_____

_____

_____

_____

_____

_____

PAY DAY IS COMING

In life there is no such thing as a free lunch. I didn't always understand this saying because I received free lunch when I was in school. What this statement means is that there will come a time when you will have to pay for decisions you made or failed to make. This is a pay day some will love and a day others will hate. If you are doing the bright thing, please stay on point. For the hustlers, slicksters, tricksters and those who have an emergency plan on how they plan to fake it until they make it (more like if they ever make it) PLEASE WAKE UP!

Here is a startling truth that many people do not know. The economy of this country does not need full worker participation in order to be strong; and you are now, thanks to globalization (learn what this word really means), are in competition with every young person your age in the world for a job. What this means is that some people must fail, become invisible, or do bid after bid because there is not enough room for them at the worktable. Is that somebody you?

You remember the chapter on seeing? Well it is time for you to stop looking and start seeing what is going on around you. See the wasted lives living and dying in the neighborhood. See all of the people who look like you that are locked up. See people who did not do well in school and now have to work in low paying jobs to make ends meet. See people who are not on drugs, are not alcoholics, do not beat their kids; many who are the working poor, who want more out of life, but still struggle to make it, perhaps, for the rest of their lives.

Do your own survey. Ask people if they had a second chance would they do something different with their lives. I bet you (if I were a betting person) that 99.9 % would opt to make significant changes. Some would probably say they would place more value in their education (80% of people in prison read under 8th grade level). While others may say they should have never started getting high, got pregnant before marriage, would change friends, relationships, or the way they think.

Do you really think all the people lost to the streets want to be nobodies? Do you think that the person washing car windows with a dirty rag really wants to do that forever? I think not. There is a law of cause and effect in both science and life. What this mean is that you are responsible for actions or inactions (cause) that will impact your life in either a positive or negative way (effect). It also mean that you can't blame other people for messing up your life even if it is true (believe me this one is hard). You have to decide how you want to live and please know not making a decision is a decision.

INVEST IN YOURSELF

No sane person would go into a bank where he or she did not have an account and demand to withdraw money. That sounds crazy to you right? Some folk are getting caught up in the game (which is not a game) by making zero deposits into their 'life bank account' yet they will stand in the 'life line' demanding what they believe is due. In fact, they want to go all the way to the 'life bank' manager's office and start screaming, and demanding to know, "where's my $%^&&*(#@! money yo"?! If you put nothing into life, don't expect to get anything out of life.

You can get mad and scream at me that you got robbed by your school, by some mean social workers, by counselors at the group home, your probation officer, or your own family who raised you wrong. You can offer excuse after excuse why you didn't get around to investing in yourself, but guess what, excuses can't pay your rent, excuses can't keep your lights on, nor can excuses put food on the table. You will be held accountable for the life investment choices (this is cause and effect in action). That is why you can't intentionally short-change yourself. Here are some reasons I have discovered why some people neglect to invest in themselves:

1. **Too Lazy** - Getting yourself together is hard work, that is why some people never bother to do it. They expect their parents, guardians, teachers, counselors, family or friends to do everything. You would not expect a person to chew your food for you, or breathe for you; there are things you must do for yourself. Here is a news flash: no one should be working harder for you than you. If you are not willing to work hard in life then prepare to be worked over by life.

   When I worked in a program that trained young people in foster care for careers in food services; I heard many why I'm late for class excuses. Some would say that it was the subway's fault. Others used the once a year excuse that they forgot to set their clocks for daylight savings time. Yet the excuse that would drive me crazy was, "My counselor did not wake me up." My response was, "Unless you can guarantee me that your counselor will be employed by you with the sole purpose of waking you up for the rest of your life, I think you should invest in an alarm clock."

2. **Born Victims** - If a person honestly feels he or she has valid reasons to throw their life away (they were unloved, used, or abused), then no human power can keep them from destroying themselves. If a person wants to drown then a life preserver is useless. People, who have been hurt, disappointed or just plain messed over, may find reasons to justify not trying, not moving, or not caring. Victims carry around in their head and heart a list of people they blame for their present nowhere situation. Rather than think

about where they need to go, victims dwell on where they have been and obsess on what won't work.

Some people willingly fail in life, because they want to hurt someone, usually a person who wants them to succeed. This is Looney Tune logic to the max. Whether you think you are a born victim, or you willingly became one, it does not make a difference. Case in point, no one really cares why a grown person fails. You don't hear counselors, teachers, or parents asking a grown person, "What's wrong, why are you riding back and forth in the last car of the train?" I am not downing homeless people mind you. What I want you to hear is that life is rough and people have a way of not seeing grown folk's pain.

3. **I Have Plenty of Time** - Schools, parents and guardians teach children how to tell time, but neglect to teach the significance of time. Think about it this way, we all have a set amount of time deposited in our 'life time' account covering the period between birth and death. If you spend most of your time wasting time, there will come a time when there is not enough time to accomplish the things that take time. Let me call a timeout because I don't want to lose you.

When a person is young, they may think they have all the time in the world to do whatever they please. What they don't know (and are not taught) is that we are not the masters of time. Time answers only to itself. When it says get started, life begins. When it says it is finished, life ends. It is our job to make the most out of what happens between life and death. I know that may sound cold, but if I sugarcoat the truth, some people will not hear it. I hope you seize the time before time seizes you.

4. **Fear** - Some people allow their fears to stop them. They fear success. They fear failure. They fear what others

may say or think. They fear not knowing what will happen if they really try (or don't try). They fear being made fun of. They fear that the negative stuff they heard about themselves may be true. These brothers and sisters have allowed fear to control their thoughts. People stuck in 'fear land' learn how to hide from themselves and others. They act as if they got it going on when all they really are is afraid. I heard that fear defined is False Evidence Appearing Real. Fear has a cousin called doubt. They can be like tag team wrestlers one sees on T.V. One works you over and then the other jumps in only to start the rumble all over again. Soon, you are so fearful and doubtful that the truth sounds like a lie and meaningful change seems impossible.

5. **Lack of Desire** - Desire is a deep yearning for someone or something. Most people understand desire when it is focused on a person or object (car, clothes, jewelry, fame etc...). Some people don't fully get that you must control desire rather than it controlling you. What is equally hard to understand is when desire is needed to get something that we can't feel, taste, wear or see like a career, education, or overcoming an obstacle. You can't go to the corner store and order four pounds of desire. You can't find desire by following someone who has it (you have to have your own dream).

There are brothers and sisters who want to be in the entertainment business but they do not have enough desire to take the first step (won't take voice lessons, won't learn how to write/spell then rhyme). There are future NBA Hall of Famers who want to go straight to the pros but don't have enough desire to try out for a local team. If you do not have desire make something out of your life, all the classes, lectures and tears in the world will not change your situation.

6. **Lack of Vision** - It is important to have a personal vision for yourself. This vision should include what you want to do, where you are going, and how you plan to get there. A vision should take you beyond what you will wear, how you look, or what you will do over the weekend. A vision should be exciting, challenging, as well as liberating. After all, this vision is for and about you. Visionless people can't see their way through hard times (and hard times will surely come). Your future is important only if you think it is important.

Have you ever had one of those nightmares when you want to run from some monster or situation and you were frozen in place? That is a horrible feeling. Well imagine if you were stuck at the worst point of your life, and could not move. That is called a living nightmare. A vision that is tried and tested will help you see your way past the nightmare and toward your dream. Now I must give this word of caution, don't get strung out on just having dreams, you must also be willing to work hard to make your dreams come true.

7. **Stinking Thinking** - Your thoughts about yourself, others, and life are important. Your thoughts direct your attitude and altitude. If you practice stinking thinking, you will develop a stink attitude, a low altitude (negative, mean, moody) and your behavior spells L-O-S-E-R. Some people don't know when they are thinking '*whack stuff.*' They may think that their biggest problem is other people, situations, or plain 'ole' bad luck. If you give up power to make change in your life to other people, or blame your situation on forces you can't see or control, you can be trapped in a world that is ruled by stinking thinking. As stated, it is important to understand that thoughts have power. A single thought can make you or break you. Unfortunately, there are too many sloppy thinkers. A sloppy thinker

is a person who won't take the time to think problems through to a workable conclusion. If you want to put stinking thinking in deep check, try to be positive, act positive, hang with positive people, and always strive to positively conceive, believe, and then achieve.

So the question on the table is how much are you willing to invest in yourself? You must decide to make a personal investment if you want to make something out of your life. Unfortunately, some of your peers may spend too much time and energy investing in other people, places and things and neglect their needs. They want to make others happy even if they become miserable, a case of when loving them is killing you.

When flying on a plane the recording always state, "Should the aircraft lose cabin pressure, you should put the oxygen mask on yourself first before trying to help others." Why do you think that is so? The answer is clear that you can't help others if you can't help yourself. Invest in you, and don't be cheap. If you want the best, then give yourself the best. Ask, are you really worth it? I pray the answer is a big fat yes!

MADD TRUTH REFLECTIONS

SECTION **3**
APPLICATION

UNCOMMON SENSE

When I was young, my mother would tell me, "Boy, you may be smart but you don't have common sense." Now she had good reason to put me on blast like that because she would send me to the store to buy a head of lettuce and I would buy cabbage. When I was told to buy cabbage, I would get lettuce. It didn't make sense to me as a child why two things that look so much alike but were different would be placed so close together. It never dawned on me to ask someone in the store to show me the lettuce or cabbage (that's using common sense). If you think you already know something when you don't, you will never be able to develop common sense. All I can tell you is that being told that I did not have common sense by my mom in turn made me want to seek it—even though I didn't really know what I was searching for.

Let's check out some life situations crying out for common sense. If you were going out with a person who is nasty to everyone, wouldn't common sense tell you not to be surprised if this person is nasty to you? If you run with a crew that steals, common sense, once again, should tell you that one day you could be busted. How about the person who is living on their own and won't pay rent, common sense should be screaming, "If you continue to do that, you are going to live on the street." Another area crying for common sense is the pull of being seen doing stupid, horrible or illegal things on social media. The lack of common sense won't allow you to care about the consequence, or if the police are checking you out, because deep down, all you want out of life is to be seen.

Common sense won't allow you to look pass the truth. I

have found that some people unnecessarily complicate their lives because they refuse to develop or use common sense. Common sense has eluded so many people that perhaps it should be called uncommon sense. See if you would agree that common sense would never allow you to:

1. Hang with people who scare you.

2. Go places where you know you can be hurt.

3. Have big fun playing dangerous games with your life.

4. Be beaten down by people who claim to be your friends.

5. Smoke cigarettes when you know it can cause cancer, emphysema, and bad breath.

6. Try to get the most out of life by giving the least.

7. Get your freedom from home by going to jail.

8. Ignore your true inner voice.

9. Try to solve problems by not facing them.

10. Have a baby in order to get closer to the baby daddy.

11. Leave your house to live on the street.

12. Hit a baby in an effort to keep her quiet.

13. Drop out of school and refuse to return.

14. Have sex with the first person who shows a sign of affection.

15. Believe being smart is to be stupid in order to fit in.

16. Treat people who love you like 'you-know-what' on the bottom of your shoe.

17. Become comfortable in an uncomfortable situation.

18. Curse out your supervisor, teacher/counselor because

they get on your nerves.

19. Be willing to die over clothes, jewelry or the corner.

20. Not study for a test and then wonder why you failed.

21. Listen to a person you know is a fool.

22. Follow someone you know is lost.

23. Ask for forgiveness and then do the same thing over and over.

24. Think you can fool all of the people all of the time.

25. Talk bad about people and not expect that people are talking bad about you.

26. Intentionally fail in order to get even with someone who wants you to succeed.

27. Let other people do your thinking for you.

28. Never say thank you to people who hook you up.

29. Believe in a person you know lies all the time.

30. Go with a player because you want a chance to play then wonder why you got played.

31. Give up a scholarship so you can stay home with your boo.

32. Know you are doing wrong and do it any way.

33. Ride in a car that you know is stolen.

34. Forget who you are and act like someone else.

35. Risk your life over some he said/she said nonsense.

36. Keep getting high and believe you can stop whenever you want even when you know you can't.

37. Steal from a person who would give you the world.

38. Have unprotected sex knowing the consequences and not care because you are in love.

39. Go against what you believe even when you know what you are doing is wrong.

40. Believe in your hustle so deep that you hustle yourself into believing the unbelievable.

41. Keep getting busted over and over again

42. Know the truth but refuse to follow it.

43. Willingly throw your future away.

44. Use drugs because you feel you will never get hooked.

45. Think you will be young forever.

46. Make the same mistakes over and over, and act like it is a new mistake.

47. Think you can change a person when you refuse to change yourself.

48. Set goals that you never intend to reach.

49. Fight hard to get out of a ditch and willingly jump back in.

I want you to return to the common sense list again (feel free to add any common sense thoughts you may have). Pick three things from this list you know you would never do. Pick three things you once did and learned a valuable life lesson (write/recite the lesson). Now pick three things that you are struggling to handle. What is your common sense telling you?

MADD TRUTH REFLECTIONS

_____

_____

_____

_____

_____

_____

_____

_____

_____

_____

_____

_____

_____

_____

_____

_____

_____

_____

_____

_____

PLEASE WATCH YOUR STEP

Have you ever thought about the steps that you must take to move from where you are to where you want to go? Well, I have this truth I want to drop on you. A step can take you closer to your goal, or move you further away. Just one small step can take you toward trouble or away from it. A step can take you nearer to your dream or closer to your worst nightmare. It makes sense, at least to me, to say, "Please watch your step." Let me drop some life-stepping insight on you:

- *Everybody who is stepping ain't always moving* — It takes more than motion to successfully move; you have to have a destination in mind. If all you want is to move from one side of the street to the other (to avoid the sun, or someone you owe money), you are moving but not really going anywhere. Where are you going in life? How are you going to get to your desired there? Where is there? Is it a hustle, the welfare line, to a job, or a career (there is a difference!)? Is it nowhere, or somewhere? Is it downtown, crosstown, or back on the corner?

- *Speaking of corners, step away from the corner* — It was there before you were born and it will be there after you die. I am amazed at people who are willing to give up their lives for a corner that will never say thanks, never take care of them, nor say don't you think it is time to move your feet. These same people are quite willing to live and die for a piece of concrete that can never know what it means to dream, love, or be happy. What the corner knows is depression, loss, drugs, alcoholism, lies, crimes, schemes, brokenness and dreams that may never come true. The corner has seen it all. Some may think they will be the first to conquer the corner. Street corners don't know how to surrender. Street corners can't express sorrow. Street corners can't die — but people do, every day on street corners all over this nation. Don't lose your life to some corner. If anything, you should vow to make enough money and buy up the block and then you can truthfully say, "I own this corner." Write, recite, or think about a response to this question: If the street corner could talk what do you think it would say to all the people standing on it?

- *Some people are stepping out of school or standing on the steps of school when they should be stepping into class (not staying in the cafeteria or hallway)* — Hear me loud and clear, you are not in school to please your parents, guardian, mentor, social worker, or your probation officer. You are in school to save your life. The world you will inherit is a no joke world. You will need either an education or a skill to compete. You can't rap your way into a job (you have to learn interview techniques). You can't fight your way in the door (with your mind, yes, with your hands, no). You can't curse people out at work and expect to be blessed with a promotion (the power of life and death is in the tongue). You can't scheme, or scare/stare your way into a position (the subway face could actually hurt you in the workplace). You must do all in your power to learn now so you can earn later!

I think you got the stepping message down pat. I don't want to overstep the issue (you know how some adults have a way of running stuff into the ground!). Now, allow me to give you some positive stepping lessons designed to last a lifetime.

1. **Don't be afraid to step alone** — Some people can't function unless they are in a crowd. There will be

times when you have to walk off and do something for yourself by yourself, like go back to school, or leave a person or group that is dragging you down. If the crowd is lost, and you are following the crowd, guess what, you are lost too.

2. **Step to your own beat** — Be yourself even if it may mean being different from your friends. You owe it to yourself to discover your true gifts, talents, likes and dislikes. That will not happen if you are always trying to be like or liked by others. Over time, you will discover that it takes far less energy and is much more rewarding to allow you to be you.

3. **Don't step over the people who really love you** — There may come a time when you have to decide if you are going to reject the people who really love you for the people who say they love you. You have to know who is for real and who is 'frontin' (more on that later). How you resolve this can determine your future. At the very least, give people who have been there for you the benefit of doubt until you are real sure who is for real. Words can be shaped to mean anything, especially if a so-called friend is trying to get over on you. A person's actions never lie, they can be misinterpreted, but believe me actions do not lie. It is more important to check out what a person does rather than what they say.

4. **Step towards the light** — You have to choose either darkness or light. If you step in the light, your stuff is visible, both the good and that which can get better. If you step in the light, you can see the ditches along life's road and avoid falling. Neither light nor darkness will automatically choose you. You have to pick your life's partner. One will mess you up and will never say sorry, or lift a finger to help you when you are down. Be

truthful, are you following light or darkness?

Each one of us has a path that we must walk (take a look at the cover—it has meaning). Some people don't want the responsibility for choosing their path and leave it to others to do it for them. It is easy to just step with the crowd but what happens if the crowd is headed toward destruction? Will you follow because you figure it does not make a difference which path to take because you are lost? That is why I found out it is important to say, "Please watch your step."

MADD TRUTH REFLECTIONS

_____

_____

_____

_____

_____

_____

_____

_____

_____

_____

_____

_____

_____

_____

_____

_____

_____

_____

_____

_____

ROMANCING DEATH

When I was four years old, my older brother and I had to move down South for a year due to a fire in my family's South Bronx apartment (on Christmas Eve). We were sent to our grandparent's home in Bessemer, Alabama. It was there that I had my first brush with death. I was playing in the backyard with my cousin. We were chucking (a Southern term for throwing) rocks at each other. If you know anything about four year olds, you appreciate the fact that they can't intentionally hit anything. Out of nowhere, I got the bright idea to throw a rock at a furry yellow baby chick pecking in the corner of the yard.

As soon as the rock left my hand, I had a bad feeling. I felt worse when the stone struck the chick and it died. I can still remember the emptiness and guilt I felt because of my action. I was a chick murderer and only four years old. I enlisted the support of my cousin and we hastily tossed the lifeless yellow corpse under the house. In the most innocent way, death became real to me.

My brothers and sisters you live in a time marked by death and dying. You see it and live it everyday. You are fed a steady diet of blended imaginary and real death, through mindless acts of violence, anger, robbery, plus new diseases and he said/ she said now someone is dead mess. If that is not enough, acts of violence can be found all over the television, the Internet and YouTube. There are people who would rather kill other people (the elderly are a favorite target) because that is easier than getting a job, getting off drugs, or being responsible. There are desperate people who are so insecure, angry and misshapen that they think nothing of blowing away someone for their sneakers, gold chain cellphone, or because of some perceived act of disrespect.

Life is too precious to die at the hands of someone who woke up angry at the world. You can wear the wrong colors and die these days. Where you were born could be the reason where you will die. If someone looking for trouble challenges you by asking, '*whatchu*' looking at, you have my permission to say, "Absolutely nothing" and keep on stepping.

A good friend of mine named Geoff Canada wrote a book titled *Fist, Stick, Knife, Gun,* where he traces the escalation of violence in the same South Bronx neighborhood where he and I were born. He talks about a time when you fought one day and laughed about it the next day. Canada clearly informs his readers that those days are long gone. Now, what are essentially petty beefs can end in a deadly explosion of violence.

What blows my mind is how readily death is expected. It is not a big thing for some folk to kill, or be killed, or so it seems. How many times do we hear that a person (child) died because he or she was at the wrong place at the wrong time? The wrong place is becoming any place. Are schools the wrong place? Is a church the wrong place? Is a playground the wrong place? Is riding in your grandmother's car the wrong place? A shoot-out occurred at the funeral service of a gang member killed by rivals in Boston, was that the wrong place? Death will never respect life even though life always submits to death.

I have met young people who did not expect to live past their teen years. These young bloods live under the shoot or get shot philosophy of the street. There is nothing more final than death. When a person dies, all of their dreams, hopes and aspirations die too.

There are some people who want to force the hand of death by making a decision not to live. Perhaps they broke up with a girlfriend or boyfriend, or they feel they can't handle life's pressure. If you think you are going to die before your next birthday, your mind can't be on what you will be doing 10 years from now.

The unnatural relationship with death and instruments that cause death have created 'punk warriors' who specialize in terrorizing women, elders, and children. Punk warriors don't mind risking their lives because they think living is harder than dying. Any fool can kill somebody. It takes a real warrior that will avoid death saying, "You won't take me out, I got places to go, things to do and people to see." Punk warriors are willing to kill, or be killed, because they feel they must represent.

What do they really represent? They represent sadness to the family who lost a loved one by a stray bullet or intentional shot. They represent an empty bed. They represent tears from a heart permanently broken. They represent an empty seat at the holiday dinner table. They represent a truly misguided lover who made a tragic decision to romance death. If you live like you want to die, then you have not really lived at all.

(Special thanks to violence interrupters around the country risking their lives so that others may have a chance to live.)

MADD TRUTH REFLECTIONS

_____

_____

_____

_____

_____

_____

_____

_____

_____

_____

_____

_____

_____

_____

_____

_____

_____

_____

WHO IS YOUR REAL BEST FRIEND?

D o you know who picked your first friend? It was not your parents, guardians, teachers or even you. Give up? It was geography. Your first friends became your partners because *'y'all'* lived on the same block. If you lived on another block, you would have had different friends. As you grow older, you have the opportunity to choose friends beyond the barrier of location. What do you want in a friend? Do you want someone who always has money (materialistic friend)? Do you pick people who can fight (protector friend)? Perhaps you choose a person whom everyone else wants to be around (popular friend). There are friends who are funny and tell great lies... I mean stories (entertainment friend). Perhaps you have online friends that you text or communicate with through Facebook, Instagram, Snapchat or Twitter (techno friends).

Can you be a friend with a person of the opposite sex (platonic friend)? You may choose a friend that will do anything for you and ask for very little in return (flunky friend). What is your definition of friendship? Best friends are a treasure and like most treasures, they are rare. A best friend is not a *'flat leaver.'* A best friend will not automatically take your side because they are afraid of getting you upset when they disagree with you. You can argue with a best friend today and still be tight tomorrow.

If your best friend is always at the center of some drama about you (which they swear on their mother is not true), you should check this friend out more carefully. A true best friend will always want the best for you and the relationship. Now that we got that out, the question that begs for an answer is who is your real best friend? Why did you choose this person? Is your friendship a one way or two way street?

If you have a 'gazillion' best friends, you may find that number is too high. One must figure out the difference between best friends, friends, associates, running partners and the 'hi/ bye' crowd. Many people who are in your life today may not be around tomorrow. Some who are your partners will eventually move away; become homeless; attend other schools; stay in the 'hood' (forever); go to college; jail; down south; to P.R.; D.R.; out West; join the armed forces; flip out; or unfortunately, they may die.

Some people I thought would be my friend forever can't be found. They did not run away, or are hiding, like when you played hot peas and butter, or, hide-go-seek (do you remember looking for your friend?). You should know that situations change, minds change, hearts change, and yes, even friends change. Remember, before being a best friend to someone else, you must be a best friend to yourself. It is your responsibility to choose wisely people who have earned the right to be called friend.

MADD TRUTH REFLECTIONS

_____

_____

_____

_____

_____

_____

_____

_____

_____

_____

_____

_____

_____

_____

_____

_____

_____

_____

_____

_____

SECTION 4
ANALYSIS

SCHOOL DAZE

started teaching high school at the age of 22. I wanted to be a good teacher who challenged scholars to give their best. The moment of truth for some of my students would arrive when report cards were issued. The ones who did poorly would usually say at the end of class, "Fonso, why did you fail me, I was here." I would tell them, "The blackboard, chair and eraser were all here too and guess what, they ain't passing either." You can never give minimum effort and expect maximum gain.

I am not trying to 'front' like I always did my best in school. That would be a lie and this book is about truth. I had to discover that giving half-effort would get you, at best, halfway to your goal. With that said, take a look at the following scenarios and see if you can figure out why some people give less even when they want more out of life (all names are made up):

Tryesha

Tryesha is 16 years old. She was an honor student in middle school, but finds herself struggling in high school. It is not because the work is difficult. Tryesha does not want to risk losing her new friends who can't match her grades. The last time she passed all of her classes, she was made to feel stupid. Several people asked her point blank, "Why do you like school so much?" It was at the moment Tryesha made the decision to lower her I.Q. so she could fit in with a crowd that could not spell I.Q. She started placing less effort in her classes; and her last two report cards showed she was being (in) effective. Tryesha was told that the boys who are really down don't want a girl who is smart. Tryesha's pride would not allow her to fail any classes. She figured if she got 70's (which is a good 25 points below her ability); she would still be able to get into college. Tryesha has her heart set on becoming a pediatrician; she really loves children.

Big Vic

Big Vic is almost 20 years old. He hates school. He hates getting up in the morning. He hates his zero period. He hates his teachers, grade advisor and the school security guard who hassles him about his cell phone and being somebody in life. Big Vic has mastered three things in his years at school: playing Spades, playing hooky and playing basketball. He would have dropped out but his moms threatened to throw him out if he left school without a diploma. Big Vic feels trapped. Most of his friends are not pressured to go to school (last night, he told his moms that he was bored by education). Big Vic wants to be an NBA basketball player. He hates the basketball coach for suspending him due to failing grades. Big Vic can't wait until he is drafted by a pro team. He wants to get far away from all the people who tried to mess him up. Every day he hears in his head his name announced at the arena, "At starting forward, number 00, Bigggg Viiiiic."

Alfonso (this story is about me)

While in the fifth grade of a newly integrated school, I was asked to come to the front of the classroom. I had to point to 7 5/8 inch mark on a gigantic ruler posted above the blackboard. The number 7 was easy to spot. The other numbers (the fraction) messed me up. I thought that if I pointed to anything after the seven, the teacher would say, "Wrong" and let me sit down. Instead, she made me stay in front of the class.

It was clear she was not going to let me slide on this ruler exercise. My classmates (who probably couldn't find 7 5/8 inches either) were laughing their heads off. Each time I pointed to something the teacher would say, "Wrong, do it again." My confidence shrank inch by inch. I was hurting and praying at the same time, "Please, oh please, let me find this stupid number." By the time my ruler-pointing ordeal was over (I never found the right answer), I was humiliated and shattered; my math confidence was at true zero.

As a result of my fifth grade ruler trauma I had a rough time in basic math in elementary school, algebra was hard in junior high, and geometry kicked my butt in high school. My geometry teacher would go off on a tangent explaining stuff about angles, sine and cosine. It seemed like everyone understood her but me. I was clueless. I would never raise my hand. I still remembered that 7 5/8 trip in fifth grade. I failed geometry and had to go to summer school. The first day of class the teacher walked in and looked us square in our eyes and said, "Geometry is thinking." I was shocked. I thought it was real hard math. He (his name was Mr. Vinegrad) started talking about the relationship between geometry and logic. I always thought I was logical, like Mr. Spock, so he had my undivided attention.

This master teacher was able to make sense out of what was previously nonsense. I saw where I made errors in the past. I soon discovered that my thinking was out of order, and by skipping, or adding a step, I threw off the rest of the equation. All I can tell you is that when I took the Geometry Regents the second time, three weeks later, I got a 96. With all that I have been able to accomplish in life, this achievement still stands out in my mind. I found out that a good teacher can make a big difference. I also discovered that I was not dumb. When I went into the 11th grade and had to take trigonometry, I turned it out. My math anxiety was over.

Some 25 years later, I met Dr. Jeff Howard, a graduate of Harvard and founder of The Efficacy Institute, an organization that helps educators teach to student abilities and not to their problems (believe me there is a big difference). His key finding is some people are born smart, but all people can get smart through hard work, dedication and mastering effective learning techniques. If you are willing to do the work and not be content to slide by, you will see a big difference in your performance.

Do you feel that you are giving your best? Is there a better, smarter, more hardworking you inside of you? What is holding you back? If you are cool with how you are handling your life please go to the next chapter. If you need help organizing your thoughts, fold a paper in half and list the top three reasons why you think you do not give your best in one column. Now next to each entry on the other side of the page, develop a plan to respond to each finding. If you stick to your plan, you will overcome mediocrity (doing just enough to get by).

If you want to be somebody, you have to earn your way to a better future. Perhaps this may all sound boring, believe me, understanding this direct relationship between effort and results could change your life. There is nothing wrong with being a late bloomer, but there is something wrong if you live and die and never bloom.

MADD TRUTH REFLECTIONS

_____

_____

_____

_____

_____

_____

_____

_____

_____

_____

_____

_____

_____

_____

_____

_____

_____

_____

WHAT'S REALLY HOLDING YOU BACK?

wish I could tell you that it is possible to live a problem free life. Every person on this planet will have to deal with problems, challenges, or situations that will mess with his or her peace of mind. Some problems that you will face may be beyond your control. I am talking about things like sickness, death of a loved one, a person you care about moving away, or being deleted from someone's Facebook page. As you can see, problems come in all shapes, sizes and intensity. You must be careful not to allow problems that you have no control over become problems that control you. You must be mindful to make sure that setbacks are not self-induced. The real question is, are you the one who is messing yourself up? It is a hard question to answer especially if you honestly believe that other people are messing you up. Let us examine how a person could be his or her worse enemy and may not know it.

Waitin' On Mah Demo

Les Moore wants to be a rapper more than anything in life. His room is a shrine to every brother and sister who made it up and out from around the way. Every time a music award show airs, Les starts to cry and moan about his demo that the studio messed up. Everybody around the way has heard his sad story. When they see him, they know he will begin talking about who blew up in the rap game. He will then give the 411 on other groups trying to make it. Les feels their stuff is weak compared to his. He will then find a way to talk about how he got beat out his soon to be released hit by the recording studio. His friends and enemies alike heard the story so many times that they started calling Les Moore, "Demo Les" behind his back.

The part of the story most people do not hear was that Les received an advance by the record company. He was supposed to finish paying for his studio time before receiving his prized demo. Les is a perfectionist and procrastinator (the type of person who waits until the last minute to do something and then finds excuses to keep waiting) which is a bad combination. Les wasted the advance money before his demo could be finished. When it was time to follow-up on the changes he demanded, Les could not be found. This went on for several months. The studio called him and tried to work out a deal to get his work out of their hands. They even offered him an internship wherein he could apply what he earned to reduce what he owed.

Les thought since they were only paying minimum slave (as he called it), that it would be quicker for him to finish the record and then pay what he owed after he blew up. The studio people would not budge. Their lawyers said, "A contract is a contract." Les feels that he was held up without a gun; meanwhile his life is on hold. He is not doing anything productive. He has some talent, but there is no guarantee that he will make it the way he thinks. After all, he is up against other talented people who are willing to work harder, sacrifice more, and follow through to make their dreams come true.

Can I Be Blunt?

Dutch loves smoking blunts. His eyes have turned a yellowish tan in honor of the smoke that clouds his brain. Dutch is slowing up and he does not know it. All of his friends who get high think and move in slow motion so it is hard for him to see that anything is wrong. When he is not smoking, he is drinking. Getting a job is out of the question and finishing school is even more ridiculous to him. Dutch makes enough money by hustling to meet his needs. He always has on the latest gear and was a good ballplayer back in the day. He got a girl or two (one is supposed to be pregnant by him) who help him pass time when it is too cold or too hot to hang on the corner.

Dutch feels that the system is set up to make him fail. He sees racism everywhere and feels justified to stand out on a corner and get high, gamble, eat, drink, and be with his 'shortie' Sheduyah because he feels that this is how to get back at the system. Dutch laughs at the youth organizers down the block who are always protesting some community injustice. He thinks they should learn how to 'chillax' like the rest of his team.

Dutch left school in the 10th grade. He told his friends the only reason the school was halfway looking for him is that he represented money. He had the ability to make it; many say that he is a natural leader and quite smart and funny. Dutch could tell you a story about a neighborhood happening and you'd think you were right there or at least he was there (which was not always the case). He also had the ability to imitate anybody. When Dutch was high, he would mimic his moms, the dean of his old school, and West Coast rappers.

Dutch blames his family for given him a get high gene. His father was an alcoholic. He drank stuff they don't make anymore like Gypsy Rose, Bali-Hai and something called Twister. His moms tried to keep the house together, but she had problems too, especially when crack took her down and then out. Dutch feels that when he is high, it calms the anger that burns in him. When he is puffing, his problems seem to go up in the same smoke and then disappear. Dutch can't think about facing life 'unhigh'; after all, what would he do to occupy his time?

Who Wants Me Now?

Amora loves boys. She has had two boyfriends in the last week. Her mother once told her that boys were going to be the death of her. Amora remembers when her mother would bring men home all the time. She would get out of bed and secretly check out the show in her mom's bedroom through the keyhole. Amora said that when she got older, she wanted to do the same thing. Amora's favorite pastime is going to the park and flirting with the boys playing ball.

She has her eye on this new guy who is wheeling and dealing on the court with his shirt off. All the girls are dying to get to know him. He is handsome, muscular and older than the boys Amora usually '*gives some play*.' She has been told that 'fly guy' has been checking her out that is why she decided to wear her way-too-tight outfit to the park. Amora knows that there is plenty competition out there. She is willing to do what it takes in order to take what he got.

The day that Amora prayed for came when mystery man spoke to her for the first time. Up close she could see that he was older than she thought (he was almost 22). He had an old beat-up car that looked like a new Lexus to Amora. Amora could not explain her fascination with this smooth talking stranger who called himself Lover D. She knew he was the one for her; later for messing with boys who could not decide if they love to play basketball more than being in love. Amora and Lover D knocked it out for two and half weeks, which seemed like a lifetime.

Amora can't sleep. All she has on her mind is Lover D. She went back to the park after he did not call as he promised. She ditched school three days in a row looking for him. She now wishes she had his real name, or an address, cell number or something. No one seems to know him (his Facebook page is no longer up). Amora tried being with other boys, but things were not the same. About six months later, a man and lady came to the park. To Amora's surprise, they had a picture of Lover D. They said that they were looking for him because he was HIV/Positive and was known for having unprotected sex with young girls. Amora heard about this HIV stuff but she thought that it only happened to people who used needles. Amora told her girlfriend that she got down with Lover D a couple of times (she could not remember the actual number). Her friend pleaded with Amora to talk to the school nurse. Amora was afraid, but she finally made an appointment.

The two health educators came to the school and told Amora that she would have to be tested for AIDS. They also told her that the virus may not show up for years. They asked Amora to give the names of all of the people she had unprotected sex with after Lover D because they would also have to be tested. When her mother came up to the school and was informed that her daughter may be HIV positive, she broke down and cried for almost one period. Amora started yelling that this was all her fault. She told her mother how she saw her with all of those men, and how she was only doing what she saw. Her mother looked at her 14-year-old daughter with tears in her eyes and yelled, "Amora, I told you that boys would be the death of you, why wouldn't you listen to me?!"

As you can see there are hidden layers to understanding why people do what they do. The fictional characters were used to illustrate how a person could be their own worst enemy and not know it. Do you know people who are sabotaging (ruining) their lives? Is it time for you to take a closer look at your life?

Can you identify times when you participated in acts that were not good for you? If you could write a letter of advice to yourself or encouragement to any one of the characters, what would you say? Please feel free to take a few minutes and write (or speak) your thoughts.

MADD TRUTH REFLECTIONS

_____

_____

_____

_____

_____

_____

_____

_____

_____

_____

_____

_____

_____

_____

_____

_____

_____

_____

_____

15

BECOMING A STUDENT OF LIFE

Most of my lasting life lessons that I remember have come after a failure. Believe me, I appreciate my success but it was my failures that taught me the most about life. It is impossible to live and not have setbacks, get backs or fallbacks. I remember the darkest period of my life (I was in my 20's). I was depressed. I was not suicidal, but looking back to those dark years, I didn't really care if I lived or died. I am glad that I made it through that scary chapter of my life. If you live long enough you will see that life is like a rollercoaster, you will have some ups, and downs, some twists and turns but whatever you do stay on the ride.

You can't fall in love with the "up" times because it will change. And you can't get too freaked out by the "down" times because it will also change. A student of life is the person who vows to learn from his or her experiences. Life is a master teacher, yet too many people play hooky from life school and they have to repeat subjects over and over again. It is something to get left back in life school. It is sad to see people who refuse to do their "life homework" (remember Fools In Da Hood?). They rather spend their time scheming on how to get something for nothing; how, in effect, to cheat life in order to get ahead in life (IMPOSSIBLE).

Please know that which cost you nothing is not worth having. If you desire nothing in life, you can have as much nothing as you want. Nothing is easy to get and hard to get rid of. Always be suspicious of programs that promise you can become a dental assistant in six weeks, a paralegal in 4 weeks, or a computer technician in three weeks. If it sounds too good to be true, it is probably not true. You should also know that any loans you take out for these types of 'rip-off' schools (some training programs are cool so do your homework by calling The Better Business Bureau) you have to pay that money back even if you drop out.

Beware of 'life-moochers' (usually life school dropouts). They want to live off you because they refuse to live on their own. Life moochers specialize in making your blessing their blessing. When you are paid, they automatically think they should receive pay from you. They have great opinions about what you should do with your money, as long as it centers on you giving them some of it. Life moochers want you to think that you will never be happy if you don't take care of them.

You should also remember the old saying, misery loves company that's why some people have to love you. If you are hanging with people who are always complaining, are discouraging and negative, I pray you get the insight and desire to raise up and split (you may also want to reread the chapter, Who is Your Real Best Friend?). If you want to be a student of life, you should know that you will never graduate. As long as you live, you should be committed to life-long learning. The fact that you are, or at least, should be growing in wisdom about yourself and life, should keep you from being bored with life. Working on yourself should be the most exciting project you can ever attempt (See Chapter Invest In Yourself).

The consequence for not paying attention in life school will cause you to get a big, fat, depressing "F" for failure. People who fail must live life in the shadows of the land of plenty. They can see people making it, but they can't have what they see. They apply for jobs, but are never called. They are tortured by the 'shouldah wouldah couldahs' (remember that chapter?). It is one thing to fail in life and you act as if you don't care; it is a crying shame to fail and you know in your heart you could have passed.

Please look at the following cases. You will be introduced to four fictional characters (once again, all names are made up).

They represent stories pulled from my work. It will be your job to analyze their situations. You should feel free to use the tools this book has provided, plus your own experience and growing common sense.

Open yourself up to see, feel and hear, even if a character is different from your experience or personality, you may still be able to learn a powerful lesson and that is what it means to be a student of life.

Student of Life Case Study # 1

One Sorry Ratched Guy

Pito grew up in an abusive household. He saw his father treat everyone in the family with total disrespect. Pito's dad would come home in a drunken rage and make life miserable for everyone. While he was afraid of his father, he would from time-to-time, have to '*step*' to him to protect his mother and sisters. The emotional and physical toll on Pito forced him to leave home. He ran away from his past but it would soon catch up with him. Pito met a girl and quickly fell in love. She grew up in a loving home. She was smart, pretty and loyal. Pito was accepted by her family and was always caring and mannerly in their presence. He felt that he had a family denied to him by his father. He was finally happy.

One day, his girl was supposed to meet him after school (she was a high school sophomore) and was 15 minutes late. She had met an old elementary school classmate and lost track of the time. Meanwhile, Pito, a few blocks away, was getting angrier by the minute. He did not like to be kept waiting, especially by his girl. When Pito saw her with the other brother, he flew completely out-of-control. He did not wait for his '*shortie*' to explain what happened; he was not in the mood for lies. He went up to boy and knocked him down. He kicked him, warning him to stay away from his property.

Pito grabbed at his girlfriend, tearing her new blouse her father just bought her. He was yelling and screaming that if she ever tried to play him like that again, he would kill her. Frightened onlookers called the police. Pito was restrained and arrested. As the patrol car darted from the curb, he was heard screaming over the noise of the siren..."Dulce, Dulce, I love you; I'm sorry, please forgive me."

Student of Life Case Study # 2

Amazing Grace

Grace was bored. She was tired of going to school, going to work and going to church. Every time she walked past the crowd on the corner, she would want to hang. She thought to herself, "I don't understand how they seem to have so much fun doing nothing." They had no bosses or nagging parents (Grace's parents were overprotective due in part to losing their oldest daughter to the streets) who enforced curfews, insisted on the family eating together, and checked to see if she did her homework. Grace noticed that the girls in the in-crowd wore reality TV make-up and amazing hairstyles. All the boys would be hitting on them even though some had babies by other girls. It didn't seem to matter. Everybody was going for self and that was what Grace wanted more than anything else—to be free to be.

Grace did not want the group to know that she was a church girl. When they would ask her where she was going, she would make up a story rather than tell them she was going to choir rehearsal or revival. Grace wanted to be down at all cost. One Friday evening after she got paid from her afterschool job, she decided not to go straight home. She saw three girls she knew from grade school walking toward the '*Ave*'. She asked them where they were going. One of the girls, who didn't like Grace, said they were going to Shaheem's house to have some fun. Grace asked if she could come. The girls were shocked. The leader of the group quickly said that this was not a place for good girls and that Grace should go on home to her mother, father and dog. The other girls laughed and started making fun of her too.

Grace was angry and embarrassed. She grew more determined to show she could hang. She said in her best ghetto voice, "*dis can't be no r-e-a-l party 'cuz y'all ain't got no git high.*" She then produced the money from her job and off they went to buy some 40's, cigarettes and potato chips. On the way to Shaheem's house, they passed two young brothers known to deal drugs. They knew what was up and decided to leave their corner office and walk with the girls. Once inside, they quickly paired off and disappeared. Shaheem took one look at Grace and knew she was going to be his (he already had had the other girls).

Shaheem lives alone and did not have much furniture except for one well-used stained mattress in the middle of the bedroom floor. He lit up a blunt and got Grace to smoke and drink. She was afraid at first, she never got high before, but he kept insisting that she hang loose. Grace started to feel free and less guilty. All she remembers before passing out was saying, "Please stop." Shaheem quickly took care of his business and fell asleep. Grace woke up. Her clothes were all over the floor. Her hair, which was always done, was a complete mess. She quickly got up from the soiled mattress. As she looked down at Shaheem through her tears, she could not believe what had happened.

Student of Life Case Study # 3

Ron Will Do What Others Won't

Rondu was in the child welfare system as long as he could remember. In his first year in care, he had seven different placements. Most people thought Rondu was moody as well as gay. What his counselors and peers didn't know was that he did not trust people because either they, or he, would eventually move away or hurt him in other ways. Rondu's birth parents were both drug addicts and could not care for him. When he was old enough, he tried to find them. Rondu always wanted to feel connected to a family—to be loved, even if his search would lead to a crack house, shelter, or jail. He discovered that both of his parents were dead. His mom died of AIDS. His father was shot by some crazy dude who had lost too much money shooting dice. The story was in the paper.

10 Years Later...

Ron graduated from Howard University School of Law. After much hard work, he made partner in a prestigious law firm on K Street. In his spare time, he funds a support group for young people in the child welfare system. Ron firmly believes that youth have the inner strength to succeed. His program is called Umoja (Swahili for unity) House. He describes his approach simply as looking out, seeing in, reaching down, pulling up. Ron has received many awards and recognition for his work in the community. While he does not talk about himself, Ron is quick to acknowledge the people who reached out to him (even when he refused to reach back).

Ron will not let young people in his charge talk, act like, or wallow in victim thinking. He was especially attentive to helping LGBT youth, given all he went through while growing up, because they are ignored, rejected and hated by so many people—including many otherwise well-meaning and caring adults. He had no problem letting members of Umoja House know that if anyone had a reason to throw his life away it was Rondu Tubman. He told his young people that after he found out that both of his parents were dead, he vowed that he would make something out of his life by turning his pain into motivation. He knew that part of his calling would be to do all he could to help any young person, gay, straight or questioning, who had to call the child welfare system their home.

Student of Life Case Study # 4

Gettin' Paid

Robert was a 'bourgeois gangsta'. His parents worked hard to make sure that their children got the best. They moved to a quiet neighborhood thinking they could run away from the forces that were claiming the lives of so many young males. Robert (called Rob by his parents and family) wanted no part of his parent's world. He rejected everything they stood for. They wanted him to be a doctor and he wanted to be a *'thug-for-life.'* Robert ran with a set that was considered "ghetto" by his peers. There was nothing his parents, or old friends could say to him about his new crew. Rob loved how it felt to walk down the street and strike fear in the hearts of young and old alike. He really got off knowing that he and his boys could make people feel afraid. Brother Robert was on top of the world until he found out that his parents were dead serious (more serious than he was) about his college education.

Sha-Rob (his street name) went away to college but

he may just as well have stayed on the corner. He failed all of his subjects. He was majoring in hanging out, drinking, sleeping, and running girls. He was kicking himself for not going away earlier. He did not have to hear his parents anymore. He could sleep all day and run the streets all night if he wanted. No one at the college bothered him about grades, or going to class. He was truly free. Sha-Rob found a crew just like the guys he left (they said son all the time too), just with less heart, or so he thought. Sha-Rob quickly became the leader of his dedicated followers. Soon, they had a bad reputation all over campus and they loved it.

Sha-Rob knew he was messing up his parent's money. In fact, they eventually ended his allowance. He hated them for being so cheap. Several days after being cut off, he came up with the bright idea to rob the commissary attendant who made the night deposits of coins taken from the heavily used vending machines. They planned their caper down to the last detail. They left nothing to chance, after all, they were college students. Unfortunately, they never heard of Murphy's Law (if things can go wrong, it will, and usually at the worst time). Their plan was to sneak up on the attendant, knock him down from behind, take the money and run. What Sha-Rob did not know was that one of his boys had a gun (that was never discussed).

When the deal went down, stuff was ragged from jump-street. The man fought back (the young thieves did not know the attendant was a former Golden Gloves champ). The brother with the gun panicked. He pulled out da nine and one shot was fired (he wanted to scare the man). The bullet tore into Sha-Rob's left side. The 'wannabe stick-up kidz' ran back to their dorm, leaving Sha-Rob on the ground crying out for help. The attendant ran to a pay phone and called for an ambulance and then he dialed the campus police.

Sha-Rob was admitted into the emergency room. The doctors worked on him through the night. He almost died three times. His parents were contacted and arrived the following morning. First, they heard the grim news from the doctor that their son would never walk again. The bullet severed his spinal column. Then the Dean stated they were willing to make a deal but their son flatly refused to identify the other participants in the robbery. Finally, the police told the stunned parents that they would have to arrest Robert, aka Sha-Rob, on charges of Rob 1. He was looking at 7-15 years.

The characters presented to you all had to make choices. There will come a time when you will have to make choices that will shape your destiny. Do you feel comfortable with the life choices you are making? Are there some behaviors you want to start doing and some things you want to stop doing? Fold a paper in half and write the words START and STOP at the top of the page. Please list three or four things that you will commit to START doing and STOP doing under each heading. Don't get discouraged if your starts and stops seem difficult. Just meditate on this thought, all journeys, great or small, start with the first step (remember the chapter on Stepping?).

MADD TRUTH REFLECTIONS

_____

_____

_____

_____

_____

_____

_____

_____

_____

_____

_____

_____

_____

_____

_____

_____

_____

_____

SECTION 5
REFLECTION

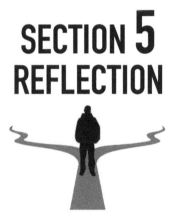

16

WILL YOU DARE TO CARE?

In this "dog-eat-dog" world, you could be led to believe that it is crazy to care about other people. There is a mind-set stating: do you and later for everybody else. I got a big lesson about the transforming power of caring when I worked at a youth program called The Valley. I sent four young people across town to help unload and distribute food for the needy from trucks full of meals for the Thanksgiving holiday. I dropped the young people off and told them pointblank, "I was not expecting to get any phone calls." Yeah, right.

Well, 45 minutes later, my phone rang. I was told there was a problem. I got in my car and drove back to 125th Street. I went inside the building. I asked the woman in charge what was the problem. She pointed to Jose and said that he would not follow directions. Before I said anything to him, I thought to ask the woman what did she mean he would not follow directions. She said that the young people were told clearly to give out one turkey, one can of cranberry sauce and one can of yams to each person on line. She said that Jose insisted on giving out three turkeys, four cans of cranberry sauce and six cans of yams to each person.

As I walked toward Jose, my spirit told me what was going on. I figured out that Jose got a high that he never experienced before. Jose came from a struggling family. He never had extra to give to anybody and now that he was in a position to help, he really wanted to give all the food away. He discovered the power of caring through the act of giving with no expectation of receiving anything in return.

Have you ever given a gift of your time, attention or

resources to a person in need? It is a good feeling, I should know, I have been getting high on caring for most of my life. I am blessed to help many people. What kind of planet would this be if we did not care about each other?

I can hear the familiar statement that life is rough and you have to do what you have to do to stay ahead of the pack. Some people compare life to a rat race. If one is not careful, he or she can become the rat in the race. People who always think me, myself and I, never talked to brother Jose. If they did, he would most likely tell them, "Even when you don't have a lot to give, you can give something."

He discovered that when you give from the heart, you get a feeling that money can't buy (remember that chapter?). People who help others recognize the warm comforting feeling that selfless giving can create. Some would call this wonderful feeling a natural high. There are many ways you can give back not because you were sentenced to do community service. Take a few minutes and come up with a plan for something you would like to do to help someone other than yourself. Here are some ideas that may get you started:

- Tutor at an after school program
- Help a senior citizen by providing one of these activities: companionship, escort services, run errands, cook or clean)
- Mentor a young child who looks up to you
- Raise money to address a problem or cause you care about
- Get friends to put on a talent show at a day care center, nursing home or hospital
- Come up with your own ideas

Remember, whatever plan you come up with, it is not for money... IT IS FOR LOVE. When you learn to become a blessing to others, you will discover that your life is also blessed.

MADD TRUTH REFLECTIONS

_____

_____

_____

_____

_____

_____

_____

_____

_____

_____

_____

_____

_____

_____

_____

_____

_____

_____

_____

_____

THE SEVEN P'S FOR:
PEACE, POWER AND PROSPERITY

I know some people whose idea of making plans does not go beyond what they will wear, who they will see, or what will they do tomorrow. The live for today crowd does not want to be pinned down by their own words. The forever *chillin'* crowd will not allow plans to "heat" them up. Unfortunately, the tomorrow I will die group live as if they don't expect to see the end of the day.

Let me introduce you to some powerful P's that can lead you toward peace, power and prosperity. If you follow the P's, your 'in-look' and outlook on life will change. The P's has helped every successful person you can name. Self-improvement writers charge serious money to people who are sick and tired of being sick and tired. I'm giving you the P's for free.

If your soul hungers and you don't know what to feed it, you should get down with the P's. If you know that you can be doing more with your life, I encourage you to hook up with the P's. If you ever, even once asked, "How will I make it in life," just watch the P's. Here are The 7 P's delivered straight to you. The P's are not magical. You must commit to them by doing the work. I hope you are ready.

PHILOSOPHY

What are the guiding principles that rule your life? I am not talking about school principals. I am trying to get you to put into words your philosophy. A philosophy is the basis of your ideas that make you think what you think and do what you do. I took my first philosophy course in my freshman year at good ole Howard University at the age of seventeen. It was at this time that I discovered the awesome power of ideas. It is important to talk about ideas, but unfortunately, too many people are content to talk about other people. If you think your life is interesting then you can never be content spending most of your time in somebody else's business. Check this out, if you got a messed up philosophy, you probably are making messed up decisions.

For example, if your philosophy is to have many girlfriends (or boyfriends), then you probably lead a life where you have to invent stuff all the time. You invent stories where girls/boys turn into cousins in order to cover your tracks. You find ways trying to be in two or three places at once. You not only have to tell big boldface lies, you have to remember what you said, when you said it, and to whom it was said. The *'playa'* philosophy will make you work hard.

Let's check out another philosophy for the sake of argument. Say you honestly believe your family owes you a living. You have no second thoughts waiting for others to wait on you. Your philosophy is endless room service then passing the bill along to someone else. This can mess you up down the line because family situations can change. A parent can be laid off from work, become ill, die, or get tired supporting a person who should be self-supporting. If you have no skills, and only a philosophy that others should care for your needs, you may wake up one day and find yourself up a creek without a paddle (that's an old saying) or in an abandominium (remember that?). Don't turn 25 years old and expect people to hear how you didn't get what you was suppose to get when you were young, causing your stuff not to take off. People do not have time to listen to adults who feel they were robbed of love, opportunity, or hope—even if it is true. Here is a philosophy that will cost you little and can save you plenty: No one owes you a living, you owe it to yourself to make a living.

PEOPLE

Who are the people you allow in your life? Look at three people who are closest to you. What are their strengths? How do they influence you either positively or negatively? If there were one thing about each one of them you could change, what would it be? As you read in an earlier chapter, you know friends can influence each other. You will do some things for a friend that you would never do for your parents, teachers, counselors or mentors. If you are hanging with a dreamless, ambitionless and shiftless (lazy) crew wanting nothing more out of life than to get high, get by, and get paid, you are already in deep trouble.

If you tell a person who is going nowhere that you want to get into a training program, get a job, return to school, read a book, or just be somebody in life, watch-out for some discouraging words from your self-appointed dream-killer. You may hear stuff like, 'why are you wasting your time trying to work because you ain't gonna get a job?' Go ahead and try it, I dare you to put truth to the test. The person who is afraid of being left behind will try to mess up your plans without your knowledge (this was called the '*okeydoke*' back in the day). They must hold back encouragement and put forth roadblocks to make sure you don't move. If misery loves company, and the company you keep makes you miserable, ask yourself, why am I still here?

PERSONALITY

Do you like your personality? Did you ever say to yourself, "I gotta change?" Your personality, like skin, will always be with you. As you get older, you will discover that it is important to know how your personality affects others. I know someone is probably saying, 'I don't care what other people think because they *ain't* putting clothes on my back or food on the table.' That statement may be true in some instances, but let's fast forward this conversation. What if you and your supervisor are having *'big beef'* and your philosophy is to curse out people who get on your last nerve; you can find yourself in big trouble. Indirectly, this person IS putting clothes on your back and food on your table because they have the power to determine if you keep your job or lose it. So, do you curse them out, or work it out? Your personality will be key to what option you take.

I recall a conversation with a young person who asked, "Why do I have to change, why can't other people change?" He was upset because he was told what he should and should not do on a job interview. It is important to know that different situations call for different responses. Just because you change to adapt to a particular situation does not mean that you are fake. Some people spend their whole life trying to change other people. They have never discovered that the only person you can change is yourself. Your personality is a direct response to your philosophy. Another way to say this is that what you think and how you act ultimately determines what kind of person you will become.

PLACE

There are some places you will never find success, peace, or happiness no matter how hard you search. I know some of you may think I have dogged out the street corner in this book. Please don't get me wrong, there is nothing wrong with hanging out as long as you know that you have somewhere to go. It hurts to see generation after generation replacing broken people on the corner like that is their job. I grew up with some brothers and sisters, who after 40 years, are still hanging on the same corner, or dying near the street corner. They look old, dry (even if they think they are still fly) and worn out. They no longer lie to themselves, saying, "I can get out of this place anytime I want." Or, "I'll hit the number and get straight." Their dreams have died and their mind, body and soul will soon follow. Yes, you can learn valuable lessons from the street.

I know this is true because I hung out (I was not born a reverend). I had to ask myself where is my place in life? I was afraid that I would not escape the street. Here I was a college graduate and was torn between going legit and loving the streets. I used to look forward to hanging out and catching up on the happenings, trying to find out who had the 'bomb;' who got busted, and who was 'giving' it up. This was the true local news and I wanted to be part of the feature story. I wanted people to say that brother must be smart, he graduated from college. He must be making serious dollars *'cuz'* he don't have to be out here scramblin' (*slingin'*). I still remember the excitement running up on a partner and greeting each other with the *'whazzupp'* outstretched hands. I thought the streets were the place to be.

I would ride around in my parent's brand new baby blue Cadillac with white leather interior *profilin'* like it was mine. I had people who liked being around me, not because I was cold-hearted (I wasn't at all), not because I was particularly slick (I thought I was), but because I had a job and always had, or could get money. One day, I had to wake up from what I thought was reality, to face reality. I had to finally see what I had been looking at for years, and ask myself, "Is this the place where you want to spend the rest of your life?" You cannot move toward a new place until you become dissatisfied and disgusted with the old place.

Describe the place where you are right now. How did you get there? What keeps you there? If there was a BETTER place for you to go, where is it? How will you get there? How will you stay there?

PLAN

The reason why some people never get going in life is because they do not have a plan. They believe that somehow, someway, with no real effort on their part, they are going to make it (remember magical thinking?). I know making a plan may seem boring, but guess what, life is not always a big party. A sound plan should have a goal and then detail how this goal will be met. For example, a person who wants to become an entrepreneur should have short range, mid-range, and long range goals in mind. The short-range plan could include finishing high school/GED and getting volunteer or work experience. The mid-range plan could call for you to go to college, or get training in the area of your interest (recording industry, fashion design, mechanic, beauty parlor etc.). Your long-range plan may include saving money to invest in your future business, owning your home, or starting a family, all on a firm financial foundation.

If you do not have a plan, it is like traveling without a clear direction of where you are going. If you get lost, you won't know it. Is it time for you to make a plan? Ask yourself, what are the three most important things I must do in order to make my plan come true? Then identify the three things that always seem to get in the way of your plans (for extra life credit, develop a strategy to address what gets in the way). You may need to become your own cheerleader when you feel discouraged. You can post positive words around you on the wall like: You Can Make It, Try Harder, Perspire And Aspire) around your room, inside of your books and in your heart. Also, seek out positive people who can relate to you. It has been proven that a caring adult (credible messenger) can make a big difference in the life of a young person (review Been There...Done That chapter). Some good places to look for help are: youth programs, some houses of worship, schools, civic groups, mentoring programs, your family, and real friends.

PURPOSE

What do you feel is your purpose in life (note purpose is an extension of philosophy and planning)? Is your purpose to have as many children as possible from different men or women? Is your purpose to use your looks to find a person who will take care of you? When you establish your purpose, it allows you to focus your energy to pursue what you desire. When you are unfocused, you tend to dibble and dabble in stuff that may occupy your time but won't move you toward your ultimate goal.

When your purpose is not clear you can be swayed by others who don't have a purpose. I admire people who say they went to the movies when they were four years old and knew right then that their calling was to be a movie director, or actor, and that is what they became in life. That was not my story. While growing up, I was a messenger, stock person in a supermarket, Vista Volunteer, afterschool director, teacher, counselor, administrator, minister, consultant, paid public speaker, and now author. I had to try different things and found that the common thread running through everything I did was helping people.

If you are searching for purpose, I can tell you where not to look. Don't look for purpose on the street corner—even if it is named Purpose Way. Don't look for purpose in people who mess up over and over again on purpose. Even if you don't know what you want to be in life, you still can resolve to be somebody in life. It is easy to spot people who don't believe that there is purpose to life. They start things and seldom complete them. They move around but never seem to get anywhere. People who don't have purpose try to lessen people living with purpose. They will ridicule them to reduce the person to their level. If that does not work, they may resort to intimidation (if you don't stop taking courses, I will leave you etc...). It has been said that your purpose in life is to find your purpose for life.

PATH

There is a path that leads to your destiny. Life is a series of unmarked crossroads. There are paths that clearly lead to destruction and hard times. These roads are not marked with warning signs yet there are signs everywhere. Look around and you can see: dead and dying people; dead and dying dreams; dead and dying spirits; all of these are danger signs. There are paths that start rough but they actually can get smoother down the line. Take the school path (please take the school path) for instance. You may not like to go to school, or it is difficult to see the point of getting up early to go to a place that you swear is boring. Here is a news flash; you will not be able to make an honest living in this world without an education or a skill. If you avoid both, prepare to be a life-moocher, beggar or thief—those are your only options. You are responsible for not only choosing your path, but you will also be held accountable for moving or not moving down this path. Look for your path, and choose one that brings you closer to your dreams rather than to some dark corner in nightmare alley. You may not know where your path begins but you must eventually discover where your road is taking you.

There you have it my brother and sister. Don't play the P's short. If you embrace them and stay with them, even when the going gets tough, you got a real shot at finding what has eluded so many people, namely: Peace, Power and Prosperity.

MADD TRUTH REFLECTIONS

_____

_____

_____

_____

_____

_____

_____

_____

_____

_____

_____

_____

_____

_____

_____

_____

_____

_____

A PLACE CALLED SOUL

You have an "inner space" where you can find truth, strength, understanding, wisdom, faith, as well as hope. Now some people may want to skip this chapter for reasons known only to them. I say, please hang in there for a minute, your patience could open up a new and exciting world and change your life forever. When I talk about soul, I am not referring to music, dancing, a lifestyle or fried chicken. I am talking about the very essence of who you really are, a glorious and divine creation that could not create itself. You are a living, walking, and breathing, miracle given the power to think; love; protect; build; create, laugh; cry and reproduce.

This place called soul can't be found on any road map. It does not reside on the corner where the 24/7 hangout crowd spend so much of their time. The Hubble Telescope can spot a universe a "dillion" miles away, but with all of its telescopic picture-taking power, it can't find the soul.

The fastest, smartest, most excellent computer can't begin to figure out the soul. The richest person in all the land can't buy it and the poorest person can afford it. I tell you the soul is deep. It can teach you things about life, about others and yourself if you would make up your mind (mind and soul are partners) to listen.

Are you with me? The power to be honest, caring, wise, patient, thoughtful, responsible and truthful lives in the soul. These qualities are activated by your free will (you have the power to choose to do or not do in life). It is your free will that will either get you up on a cold morning, or tell you to stay under the covers. It is free will that gives you the strength to want to learn and accept hard truths. Just like we all are different in shapes, sizes and colors, an individual's free will can also vary.

The good thing about the soul is that its inner qualities can be developed. You can become more caring, more honest, more respectful, more insightful and more truthful. You have been given free will to become what you want to be in life. It is your sole (soul) responsibility to use your freedom to choose wisely. The more you learn about yourself, the more you will want to know. When the desire to know overtakes your lack of self-knowledge, this is the glorious beginning of insight. This is when you can truly become a student of life. My wish for you is that you burn with a desire, to first find, then get to know, and then love yourself way down deep in your soul.

MADD TRUTH REFLECTIONS

_____

_____

_____

_____

_____

_____

_____

_____

_____

_____

_____

_____

_____

_____

_____

_____

_____

_____

A LOVE SUPREME

I want to tell you the truth about love. I know some of you may say you already know all there is to know about it. Do you really? Love has two reputations. Love is blamed for many things that go wrong in a person's life. The lack of parental love contributes to low self-esteem, low-achievement, low-aim and low-living. Love has taken the rap for breaking hearts. Love has been used to con people out of valuables by emotional hustlers. Love has been linked to people who disgrace themselves in public over some mess that should've stayed private. It makes one wonder if love is a good thing or not?

Have you ever been in love (some should say, "I lust you" rather than I love you)? Have you ever looked deep in the eyes of another person and saw everything that you ever wanted? How did you learn about love, was it from the movies, books, online streaming, videos, or television? Did you learn about love through trial and error; from what you experienced at home, or in the street?

When someone plays "games" with somebody's affection, and fools them by acting all sincere, it is usually love that is blamed and not the 'playa-playa.' People who have been hurt in a relationship may say things like, "I will never love again— it's too painful," or they may vow, "To hurt the next person before they hurt me." Love was never meant to be a destructive weapon.

If love was a precious diamond, would you give it away to any and everybody who came along and asked you for it (you would want to check the person out—right?)? I have discovered that what a person will do with something of little value is a reliable indicator of what they will do with something of greater value. Let me see if I can break this down, not because you are not getting it, but because I want to make sure you are getting it.

Let's say a person asks to borrow a $100.00 and you tell him that you don't have that much, but you have $5.00 which must be repaid on a certain date. If the person is honest, he will bring back the $5.00. If the person is *gamin,*' he will try to avoid you. If he bumps into you and doesn't have the cash, be prepared to hear one $5.00 excuse after the other. If you are following this thought, you probably see the common sense in making a $5.00 'like' investment before making a $100.00 'love' investment (this is hardcore street mathematics).

There is a Love Supreme and it is as rare as a diamond, but once found, it has the power to enrich your mind, body and soul. This Love Supreme must be shared because that is how it grows. This type of Love can't be used to play a person. This Love Supreme is pure. Dirty hands have to go somewhere and wash before touching it. Love Supreme will make a person willingly sacrifice for another with no expectation of getting anything in return (remember that chapter?).

Love Supreme is not crude, lewd or rude. It won't say, 'Ohhh baby baby' late at night and say '%^$$**' you' during the day. Love Supreme will cause you to value yourself and others even when folk act in a manner that makes '*ya wanna holla.*' Love Supreme is so precious no one should waste it playing games. It can move strangers to care about each other. It has the power to make one forgive, forget and forge onward.

Some skeptical folk will argue that there is no such thing as Love Supreme. They can present case after case where love has fallen short causing deep hurt as proof. All I can say is that they can't possibly know what they have not experienced. Many people have cut themselves off from love because of what they mistakenly thought was love.

There are some brothers and sisters wondering where do I

find Love Supreme? You don't have to go out and find it because Love Supreme is already looking for you. Before it can dwell inside of you, there is a task of emptying out what is broken, negative, useless, messy, or stink that is taking up valuable space. Then you can make room for what is pure, joyous, forgiving, hopeful, and true. The more mess you empty out, the more room you have for a refill; and don't be afraid to take as much as you want. Love Supreme will never run out nor run away. Now you are ready. Picture yourself as a glass before a fountain. What things will you empty out? What things will you want to fill up?

I know this probably sounds too fantastic to be true, like some science fiction movie or something. You should know there are people, not everyone mind you, who have been searching for Love Supreme that has the awesome power to bring peace of mind and transformation. They have to believe it exists so that they can exist. Beloved, do not be afraid to search for Love Supreme. I am a living witness who can say that after a real encounter, you will never be the same, and that is *Madd Truth*.

MADD TRUTH REFLECTIONS

_____

_____

_____

_____

_____

_____

_____

_____

_____

_____

_____

_____

_____

_____

_____

_____

_____

_____

_____

_____

MADD TRUTH WISDOM SAYINGS

1. *People who really love you will speak the truth to you, even if it hurts.*

2. *You will meet people who are not what they appear to be, it is your job to keep looking until you see the real person.*

3. *Insight is a gift that can help you stop looking at others and start seeing yourself.*

4. *What is pleasing to the eye may not always be pleasing for you.*

5. *It is impossible to help a person who can't see any need for help.*

6. *A smart way to positively impact your future is to successfully learn from your past.*

7. *Forgiveness is not about who was right or wrong; it means you are ready to move on with your life.*

8. *If the past is a drag, and it is not serving you well, you have the right to ask why am I serving it?*

9. *Think of yourself as an unfinished work of art and vow to keep on painting until the masterpiece is done.*

10. *Do not put your life on hold while waiting for the right time to get yourself together. The right time is NOW!*

11. *Your past is not holding you back-check it out, the past has no hands.*

12. When you were a child, you thought as a child, you reasoned as a child, you acted and reacted as a child, but if you are to mature, you have to make a decision to put away childish things.

13. We tell ourselves lies, but it does not change the truth it just postpones it for a while.

14. Not one person who draws breath can truthfully say that he or she made it alone—everybody needs help such as a word of encouragement; support or just a friendly ear.

15. Your thoughts have power that is precisely why you must be mindful of what is on your mind.

16. No one makes a plan to ruin his or her life; in most cases it is a slow slide down a slippery pole.

17. You may have fallen—even been knocked down, but it is your responsibility, your duty to get up, dust yourself off, learn from your mistakes, and get going.

18. If you do not have desire to make something out of your life, all the classes, lectures and tears in the world will not change your situation.

19. Choices made from desperation usually come back to haunt you.

20. If you want wisdom, go to the wise, if you want to be fooled, go to a fool.

21. You will be older a lot longer than you will be young.

22. There is very little that is new under the sun just new thoughts about old things.

23. Money can change the external, but it will not automatically change the internal.

24. In life there is no such thing as a free lunch.

25. *You are responsible for actions or inactions (cause) that will impact your life in either a positive or negative way (effect).*

26. *If you put nothing into life, don't expect to get anything out of life.*

27. *Not making a decision is a decision.*

28. *Excuses can't pay your rent, excuses can't keep your lights on, nor can excuses put food on the table.*

29. *No one should be working harder for you than you.*

30. *If a person wants to drown then a life preserver is useless.*

31. *If we spend most of our time wasting time, there will come a time when there is not enough time to accomplish the things that take time.*

32. *Seize the time before time seizes you.*

33. *Your future is important only if you think it is important.*

34. *Don't get strung out on just having dreams, you must also be willing to work hard to make your dreams come true.*

35. *Be positive, act positive, hang with positive people, and always strive to positively conceive, believe, and then achieve.*

36. *You can't help others if you can't help yourself.*

37. *If you think you already know something when you don't, you will never be able to develop common sense.*

38. *You must do all in your power to learn now so you can earn later!*

39. *It takes far less energy and is much more rewarding to allow you to be you.*

40. *It is more important to check out what a person does rather than what they say.*

41. *Death will never respect life even though life always submits to death.*

42. *If you live like you want to die, then you have not really lived at all.*

43. *A true best friend will always want the best for you and the relationship.*

44. *It is your responsibility to choose wisely people who have "earned" the right to be called friend.*

45. *You can never give minimum effort and expect maximum gain.*

46. *Some people are born smart, but all people can get smart through hard work, dedication and mastering effective learning techniques.*

47. *There is nothing wrong with being a late bloomer, but there is something wrong if you live and die and never bloom.*

48. *Be careful not to allow problems that you have no control over become problems that control you.*

49. *Life is a master teacher, yet too many people play hooky from life school and they have to repeat subjects over and over again.*

50. *Please know that which cost you nothing is not worth having.*

51. *If it sounds too good to be true, it is probably not true.*

52. *Misery LOVES company that's why some people have to love you.*

53. *If you want to be a student of life you should know that you will never graduate.*

54. *All journeys, great or small, start with the first step.*

55. *Even when you don't have a lot to give, you can give something.*

56. *When you learn to become a blessing to others, you will*

discover that your life is also blessed.

57. No one owes you a living, you owe it to yourself to make a living.

58. The only person you can change is yourself.

59. What you think and how you act ultimately determines what kind of person you will become.

60. I could not move toward a new place until I became dissatisfied and disgusted with the old place.

61. It has been said that your purpose in life is to find your purpose for life.

62. Even if you don't know what you want to be in life, you still can resolve to be somebody in life!

63. You are responsible for not only choosing your path, but you will also be held accountable for either moving or not moving down this path.

64. You may not know where your path begins, but you must eventually discover where your road is headed.

65. You have been given free will to become what you want to be in life—it is your sole (soul) responsibility to use your freedom to choose wisely.

66. Burn with a desire, to first find, then get to know, and then love yourself way down deep in your soul.

67. What a person will do with something of little value is a reliable indicator of what they will do with something of great value.

68. Many people have cut themselves off from love because of what they mistakenly thought was love.

69. There is inner recovery through self-discovery.

CLOSING
THOUGHTS

can't tell you how happy I am that you (and I) got to this part of the book. Please know that I tried, to the best of my ability, to present a reality that readers could relate to, learn from and be challenged by. Looking back over the different chapters, I laughed, reflected and sometimes cried. I came so close to giving my future away because I thought my change would never come. I wish I could have read a book like this when I was young (what is scary is that I may have blew it off). If you think that *Madd Truth* could help a person who is struggling with life, please turn the person on to the book.

I visualize *Madd Truth* cipher sessions where young people and credible messengers come together to share their life experiences, thoughts, fears and triumphs. I have spent my life putting countless thousands of young people in the lifeboat. The truth is that there are still too many people drowning in plain view of people who, for whatever reason, will not lend a hand. If you are in deep water, I pray that this book shows you how to swim, and that you in turn, become good at rescuing others who may be drowning. Please know there is inner recovery through self-discovery.

Most of the scenarios and case studies that you read came from my personal and professional experience. I did use creative license to make the "life lessons" pop out. I tried to blend humor, insight and complexity, along with some of the contradictions that make life both fascinating and difficult at the same time. What it also is important to say that you shouldn't go through life expecting truth to jump from behind a bush and attack you. You should enjoy growing up for there will never be another time like this in your life. Your young years should be a special time of preparation, a time for discovery and a time to develop the awesome potential inside of you. So live, have fun and keep your wise eyes open so you can see (and not just look) real people, straight-up places and embrace healthy thoughts... '*aigghht!?*'

So now, a bittersweet moment, I must say later to you. Please know that you are now full-fledged students of life. I hope you will be able to respond honestly to truth and other life challenges as you encounter it in your mind, heart and soul. This does not mean that you will not have problems. A student of life I met while doing a workshop at a local college had a hard time growing up. He said one of his mentors told him, "Just because you had problems does not mean you become a problem." Keep on studying life and yourself; and always remember that you will never run out of material. I want to close by thanking all of the young people who helped me grow up while they were growing up. Peace.

WHAT IF

What if
you are here for more
your life existence
purpose is about
more than the block
more than your peoples
more than the last thing
that got you tight

What if
you are the difference
you are the change
you are worth more
than the lyrics you spit

What if
you are destined
for even more
than the next song
to be dropped
You are not
a mistake
you were created
to be free
your life
has incredible value
we are all waiting
for

who you are to become
There are things
that cannot happen
in this world
it's waiting for you
to do it
There are dreams
waiting
for reality
you are the example
we need to see first

What if
you are not yet
all you are going to be

What if
Just when it seems
like there is
no more hope
Just think

What if?

*- Ayanna M. Cole, Manager,
NeON Arts, Carnegie Hall*

DR. ALFONSO WYATT

Dr. Alfonso Wyatt is a renowned public theologian, role model, mentor and national speaker on issues that impact children, youth, families and community health. He is an advisor to government, universities, public schools, community-based organizations and civic groups. He is an Ordained Elder on the ministerial staff of The Greater Allen AME Cathedral of New York. He has designed innovative workshops, retreats and seminars for church leaders, men, youth ministries and married couples. Alfonso Wyatt attended Howard University, Columbia Teachers College, The Ackerman Institute for Family Therapy, Columbia Institute for Nonprofit Management, and New York Theological Seminary, serving as an adjunct professor, program advisor and member of The Board of Trustees.

OTHER BOOKS BY DR. ALFONSO WYATT

Dr. Alfonso Wyatt's books are available on **Amazon.com**, **Barnes and Noble** online and all additional major online stores.

Strategic Destiny
DESIGNING FUTURES THROUGH FAITH & FACTS